Funny Bums

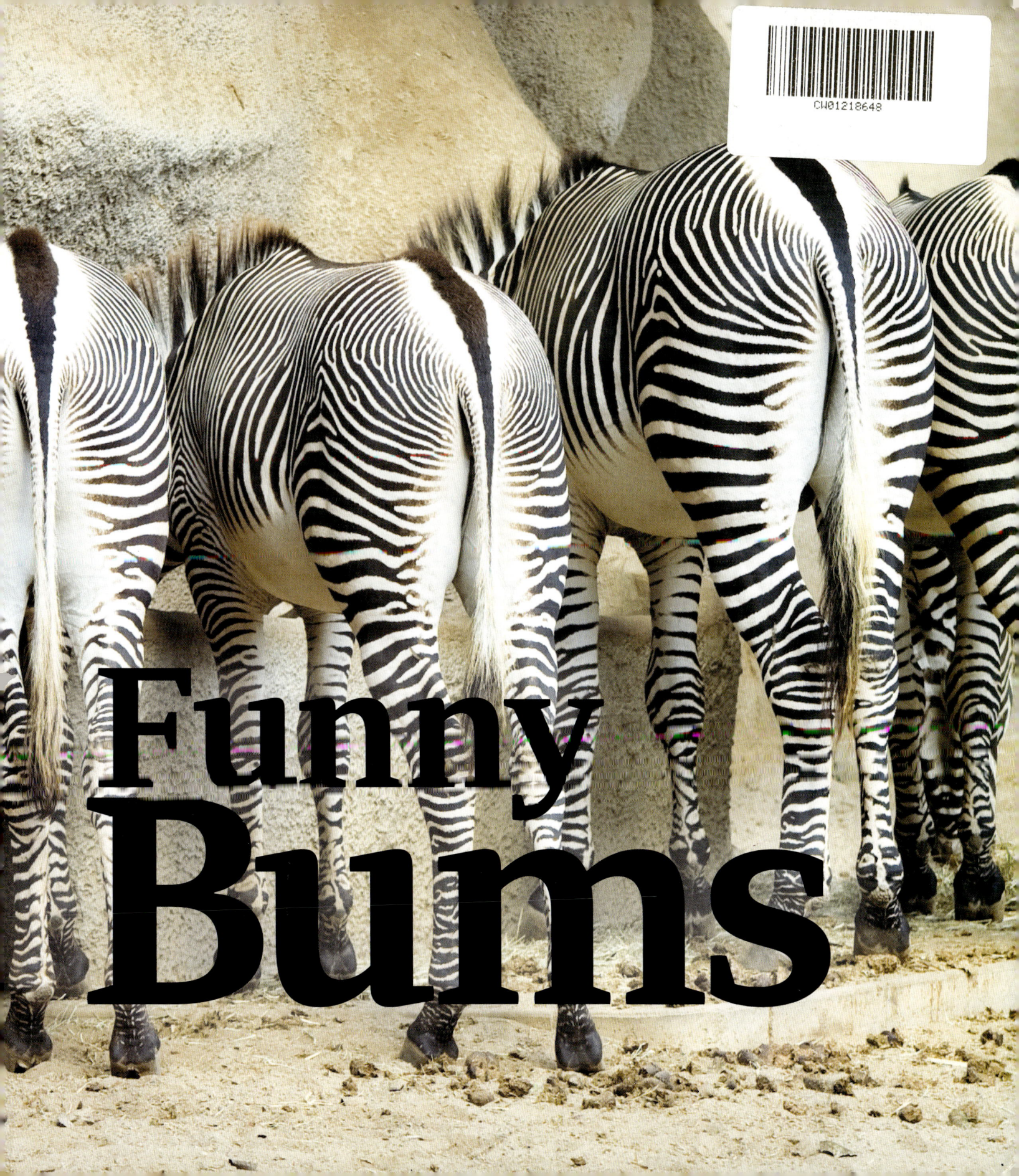

First published in 2013
by black dog books,
an imprint of Walker Books Australia Pty Ltd
Locked Bag 22, Newtown
NSW 2042 Australia
www.walkerbooks.com.au

The moral rights of the author have been asserted.

Text © 2013 Mark Norman

All rights reserved. No part of this publication may be reproduced, stored in a retrieval system, or transmitted in any form or by any means – electronic, mechanical, photocopying, recording or otherwise – without the prior written permission of the publisher.

National Library of Australia Cataloguing-in-Publication entry:
Norman, Mark Douglas
Funny bums / Mark Norman.
ISBN: 978 1 742032 50 4 (pbk.)
For primary school age
Subjects: Animal communication.
        Animal defenses.
591.59

Typeset in Adobe Garamond Pro and Adamant BG

Printed and bound in China

10 9 8 7 6 5 4 3 2 1

Image credits: front cover (elephant) © **iStockphoto.com/ShootOutLoud**; back cover (ducks) © **Peteri/Shutterstock.com**; p1 (zebras) © **J. Cameron Gull/Shutterstock.com**; p2 (peacock), p3 (porcupine), p5 (baboon, bulldog), p10 (peacock), p18 (caterpillar), p19, p31 (skunk), p22 (scorpion) © **Eric Isselée/Shutterstock.com**; p4 (fish) © **bluehand/Shutterstock.com**; p5 (turkey) © **Jeff Banke/Shutterstock.com**; p6 (grasshopper) © **Museum of Victoria, Julian Finn**; p7, p30 (rattlesnake) © **Audrey Snider-Bell/Shutterstock.com**; p8 (spider) © **Mirvav/Shutterstock.com**; p9, p31 (trapdoor) © **Museum of Victoria, Mark Norman**; p11 (lemurs) © **Jan Zoetekouw/Shutterstock.com**; p12 (monkey) © **worldswildlifewonders/Shutterstock.com**; p13, p30 (seahorse) © **Evocation Images/Shutterstock.com**; p14 (shark) © **TsuneoMP/Shutterstock.com**; p15 (dolphin) © **Willyam Bradberry/Shutterstock.com**; p16, p30 (bombardier beetle) © **National Academy of Sciences, U.S.A.**; p17, p31 (sea cucumber) © **Gary Bell/Oceanwide Images**; p20, p32 (bees) © **Katrina Brown/Shutterstock.com**; p21 (bull ant) © **Peter Waters/Shutterstock.com**; p23 (stingray), p31 (whale shark) © **Krzysztof Odziomek/Shutterstock.com**; p24 (porcupine) © **MartinMaritz/Shutterstock.com**; p25 (stegosaurus skeleton) © **Linda Bucklin/Shutterstock.com**; p26 (goanna) © **Juha Sompinmäki/Shutterstock.com**; p27, p31 (gecko) © **Museum of Victoria, Mark Norman**; p28 (snail) © **vnlit/Shutterstock.com**; p29, p30 (sea anemone) © **Museum of Victoria, Mark Norman**.

Funny Bums

Dr Mark Norman

black dog

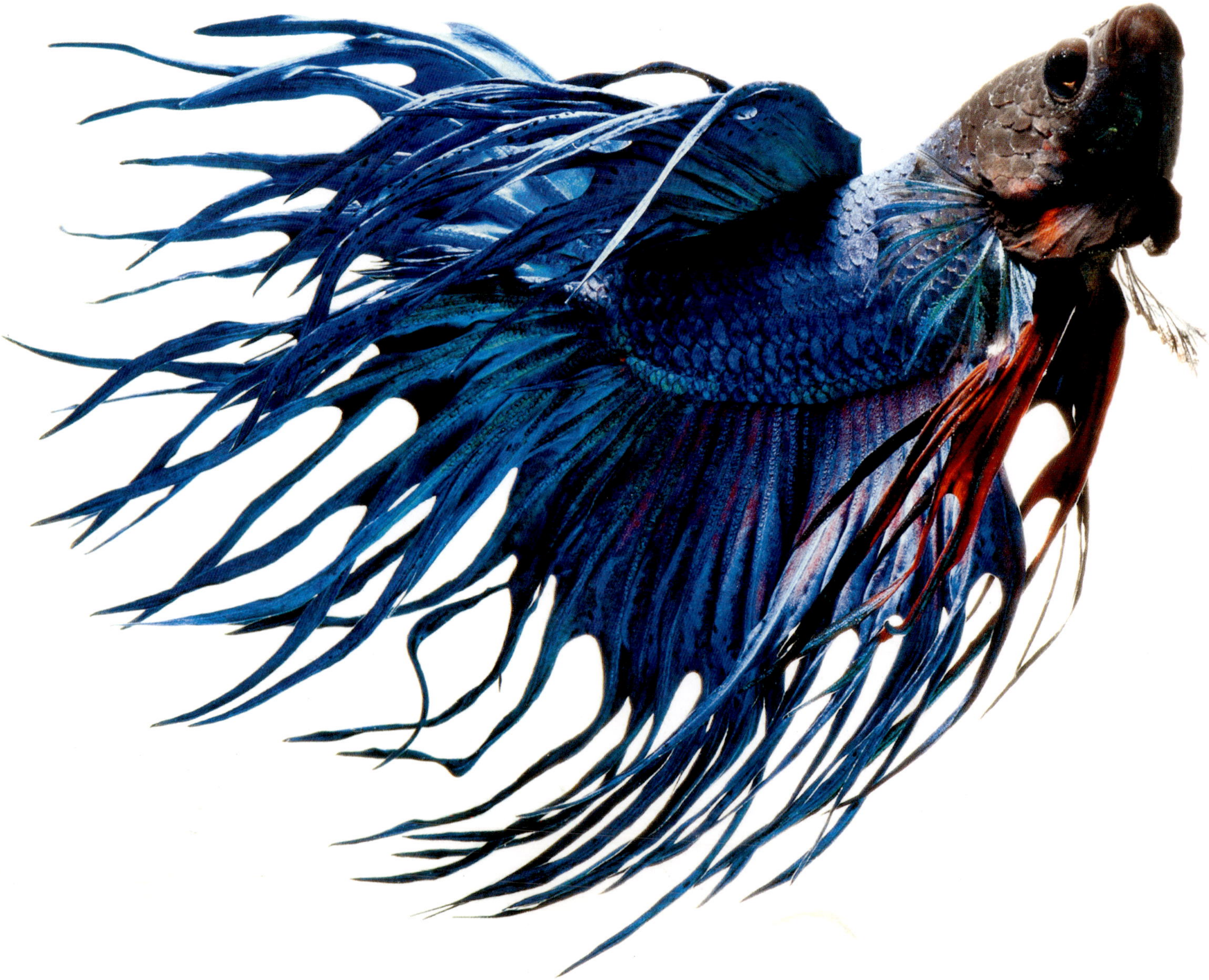

Different bums

Different animals have different bottoms. Some animals have tails, some don't. For some animals it's hard to work out where the bums are!

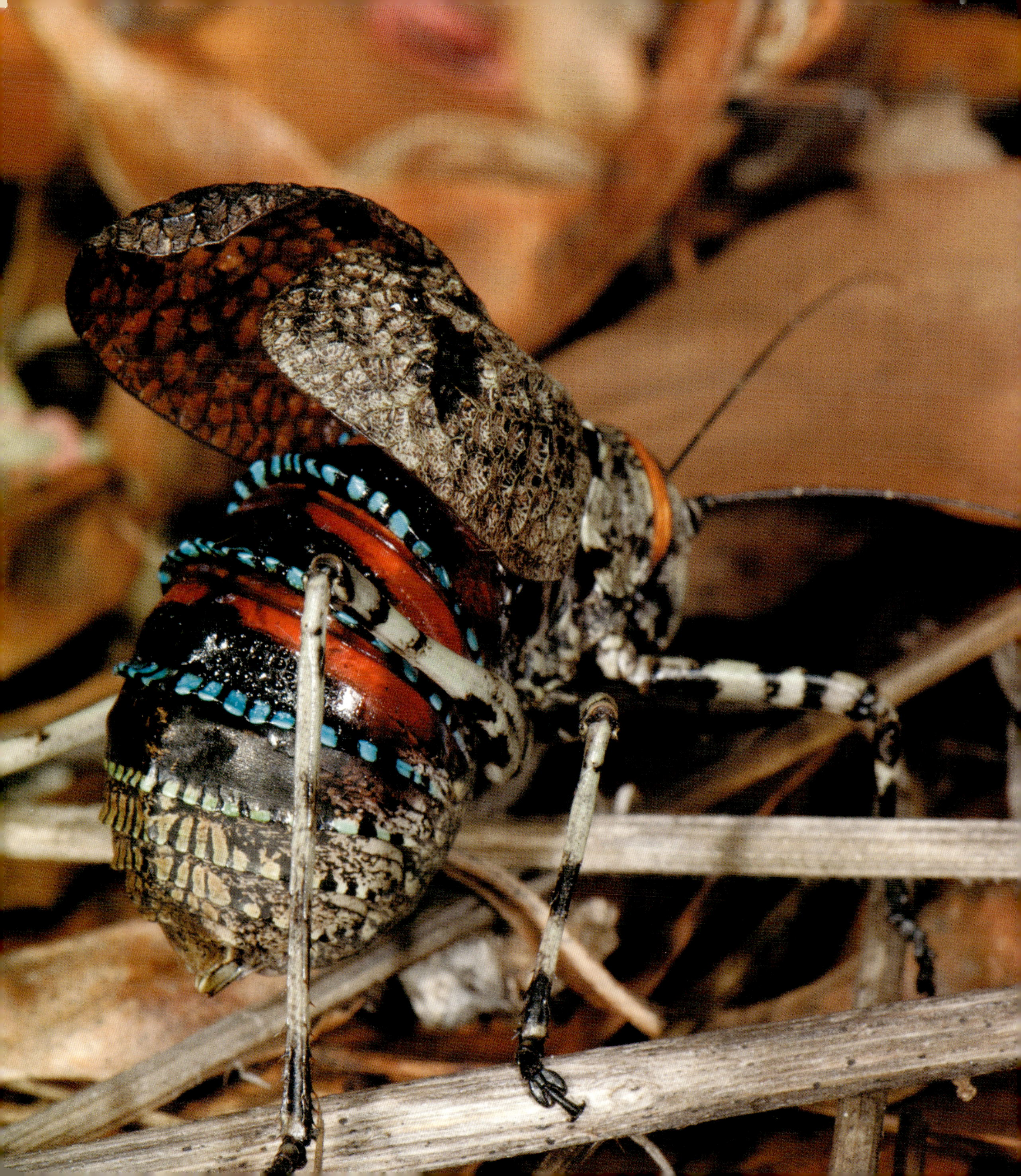

Scary bums

Some animals are poisonous to eat and they let attackers know with bright colours. The bright bum of this poisonous grasshopper warns birds not to eat it.

A special group of venomous snakes have tails that make sounds to warn off other animals.

Rattlesnakes have special hollow scales at the tips of their tails that rub against each other to make loud sounds like a child's rattle.

Spinning webs

Most spiders have little glands on their tails called spinnerets, from which they pull threads of sticky silk. Some spiders use this silk to make big webs to catch flying insects. Some big spiders can even catch and eat birds!

Trapdoors and trip-wires

Trapdoor spiders use the silk from their tails to make burrows with special hidden doors. They spread threads of web over the ground – just like trip-wires. When an insect trips on a thread, the spider feels it and leaps out to grab its dinner.

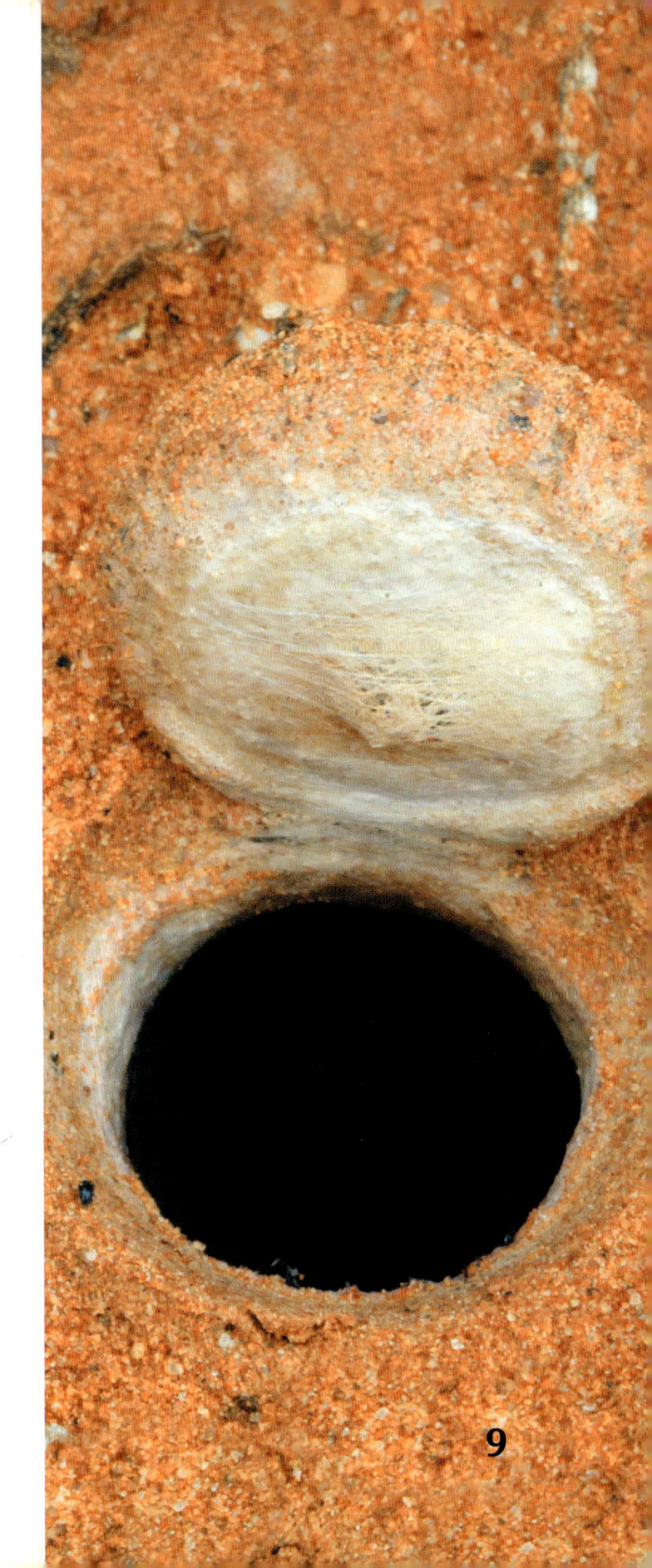

Flashy tails

Some animals use their tails to talk to their own kind.

Male peacocks spread out their amazing tails to impress female peacocks.

Lemurs have long banded tails, which means family members can always see each other when out hunting in the forest.

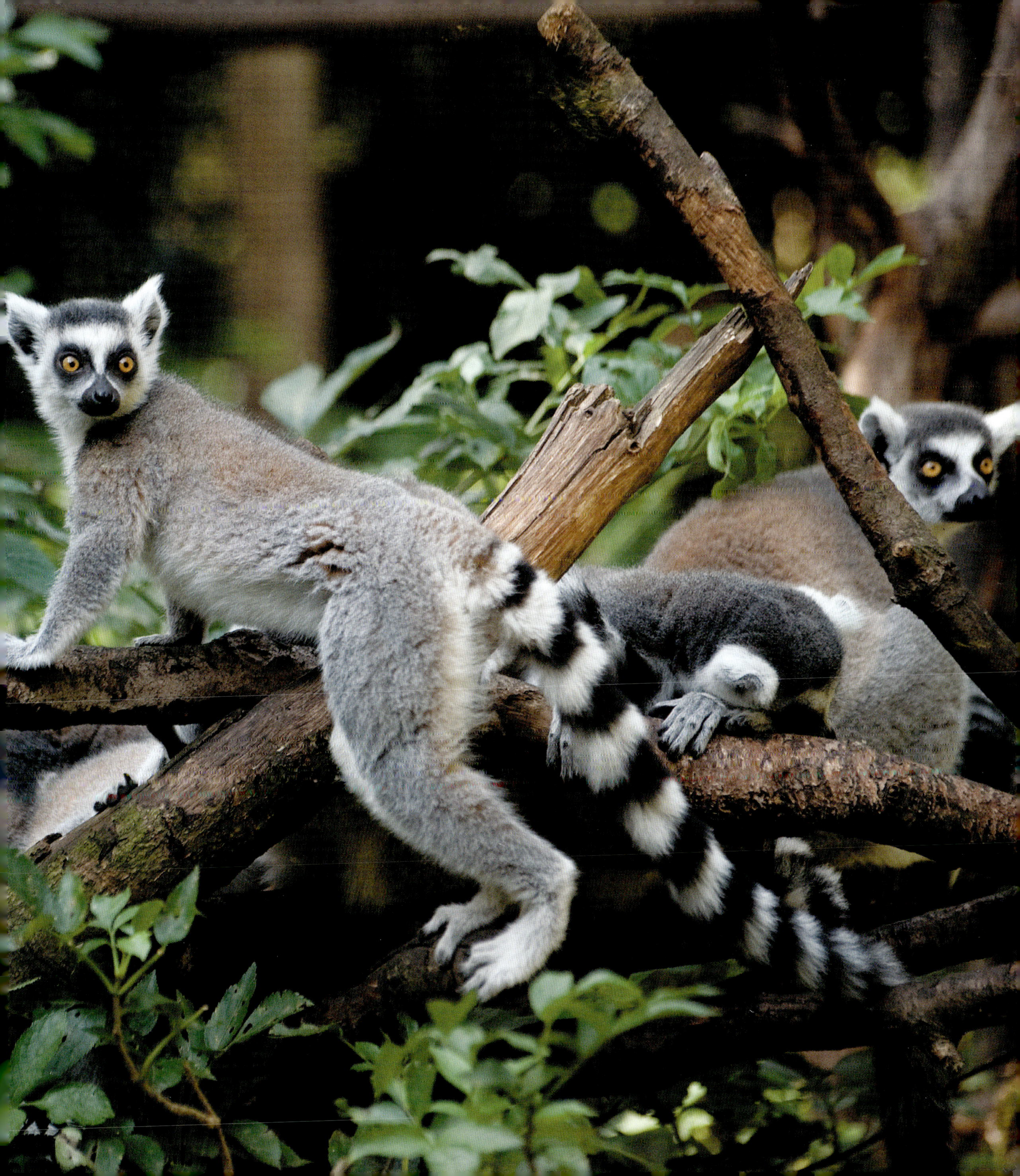

Tails for hanging on

A tail that can grip onto things such as a branch is known as a prehensile tail.

Many monkeys use their prehensile tails like a fifth leg so they can move quickly through the treetops.

Seahorses are fish that have no fins on the end of their long bendy tails. Instead they use their tails to hold onto seaweed or coral.

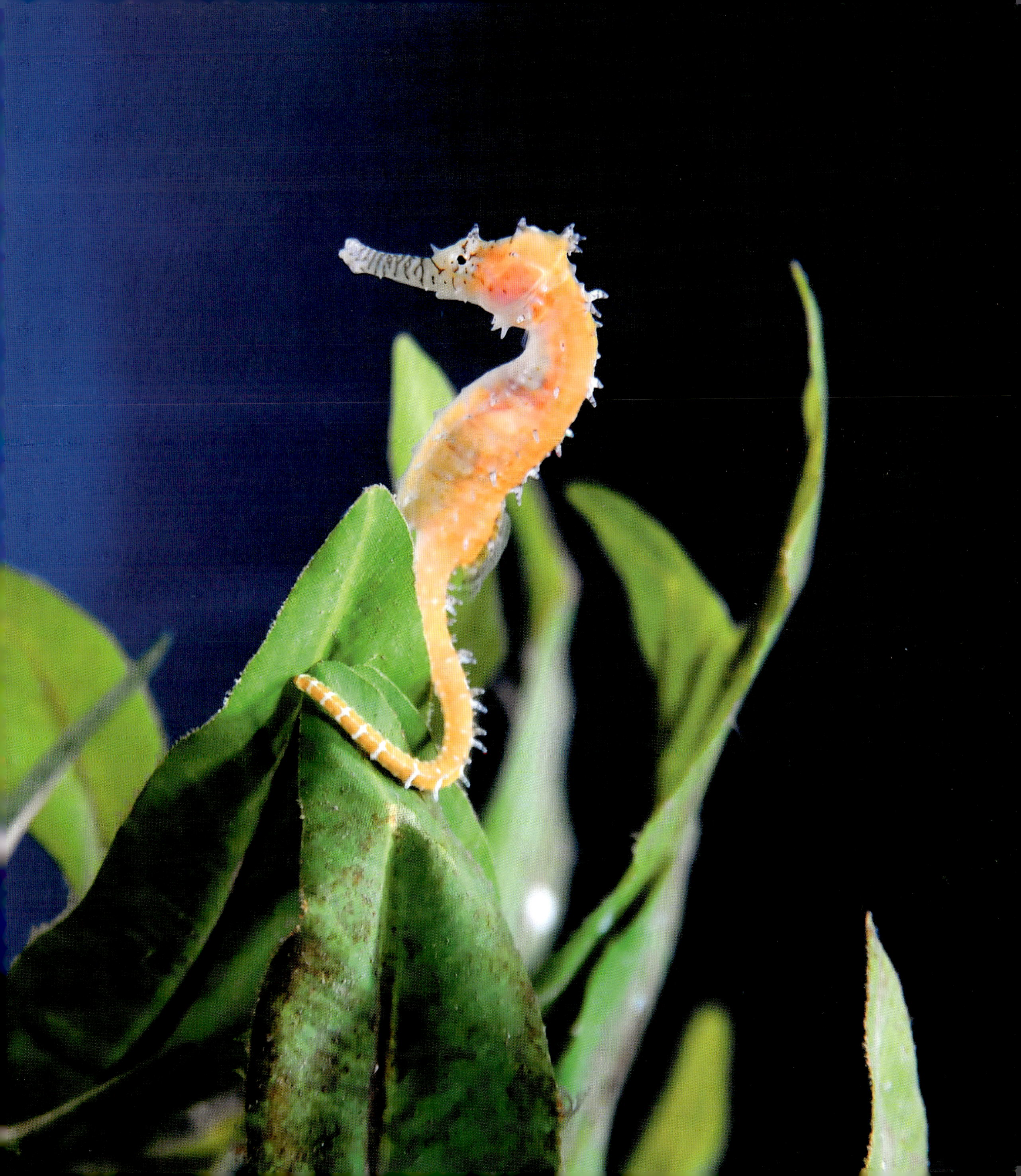

Swimming tails

Flat tails are useful for swimming. The tails of sharks and other fish are upright and go from side to side. This lets them swim fast while staying at the same depth.

The tails of whales and dolphins lie flat and go up and down. This is so they can easily swim to the surface when they need to breathe.

Exploding bums

Bombardier beetles have bums like cannons. They mix chemicals in their tails to make boiling hot explosions of liquid that can burn attackers.

Sticky bums

When attacked, sea cucumbers squirt sticky threads of glue out of their bottoms. The glue spaghetti sticks to the faces of their attackers.

Smelly bums

Both caterpillar and adult stink bugs can squirt horrible-smelling liquids from their rears. Some of the chemicals are so nasty that they can even kill a bird.

If attacked, skunks also squirt liquid from under their tails. The stink is like rotten eggs, garlic and burnt rubber all mixed together.

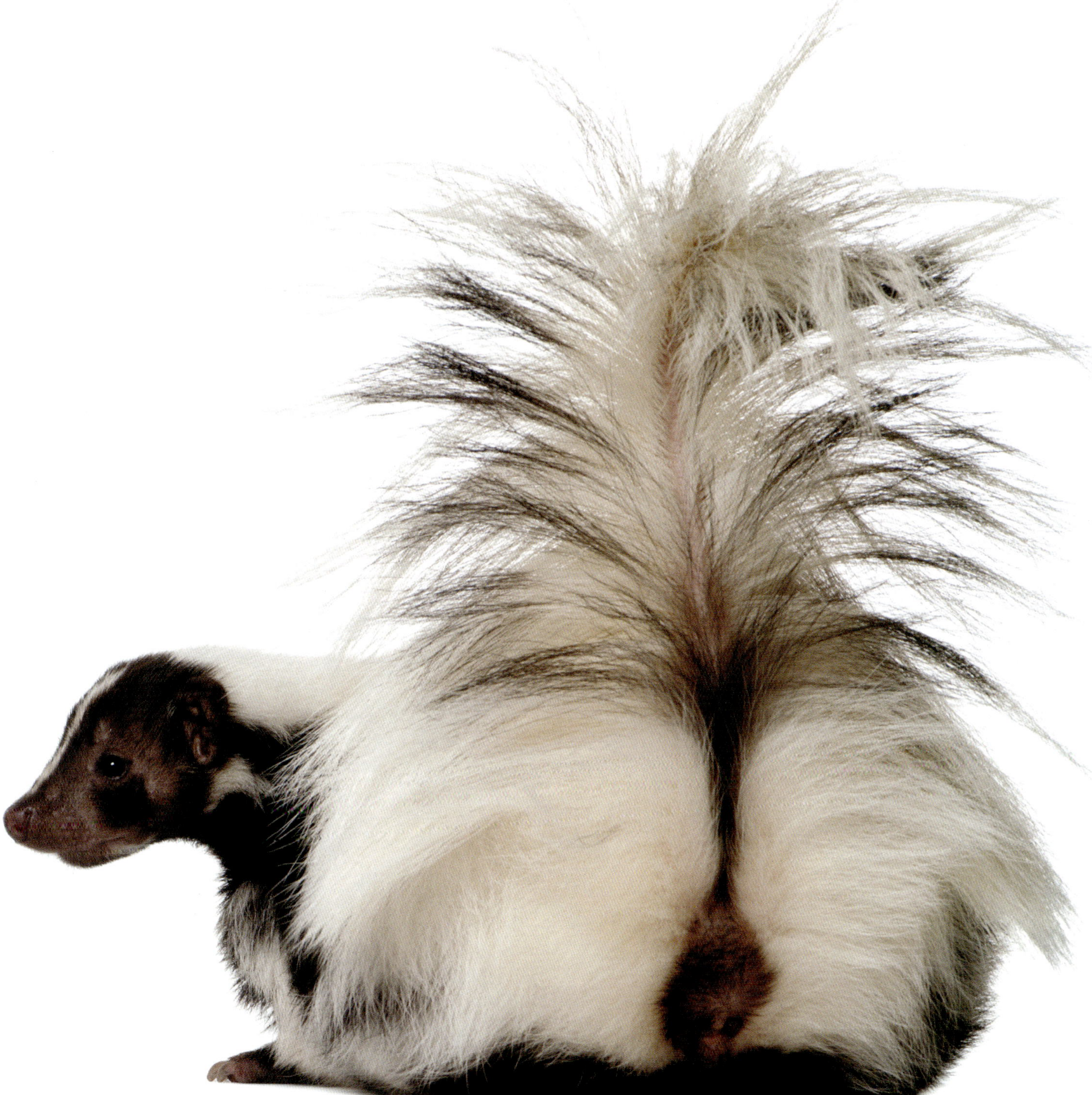

Sting in the tail

Bees have painful stings in their tails that they use to protect the hive. Only the female worker bees and the queen bee have stings.

It's not the bite of this bull ant that is painful, it's the poisonous sting in its tail. The jaws are only used for fighting other ants and carrying food.

Jabbing and stabbing

Scorpions have poisonous stings on the tips of their tails. They catch animals with their claws and quickly jab them with their stings to paralyse them.

Stingrays have one or two sharp poisonous spines on their tails. If attacked, they whip their tails up over their bodies and drive the spines into the attackers.

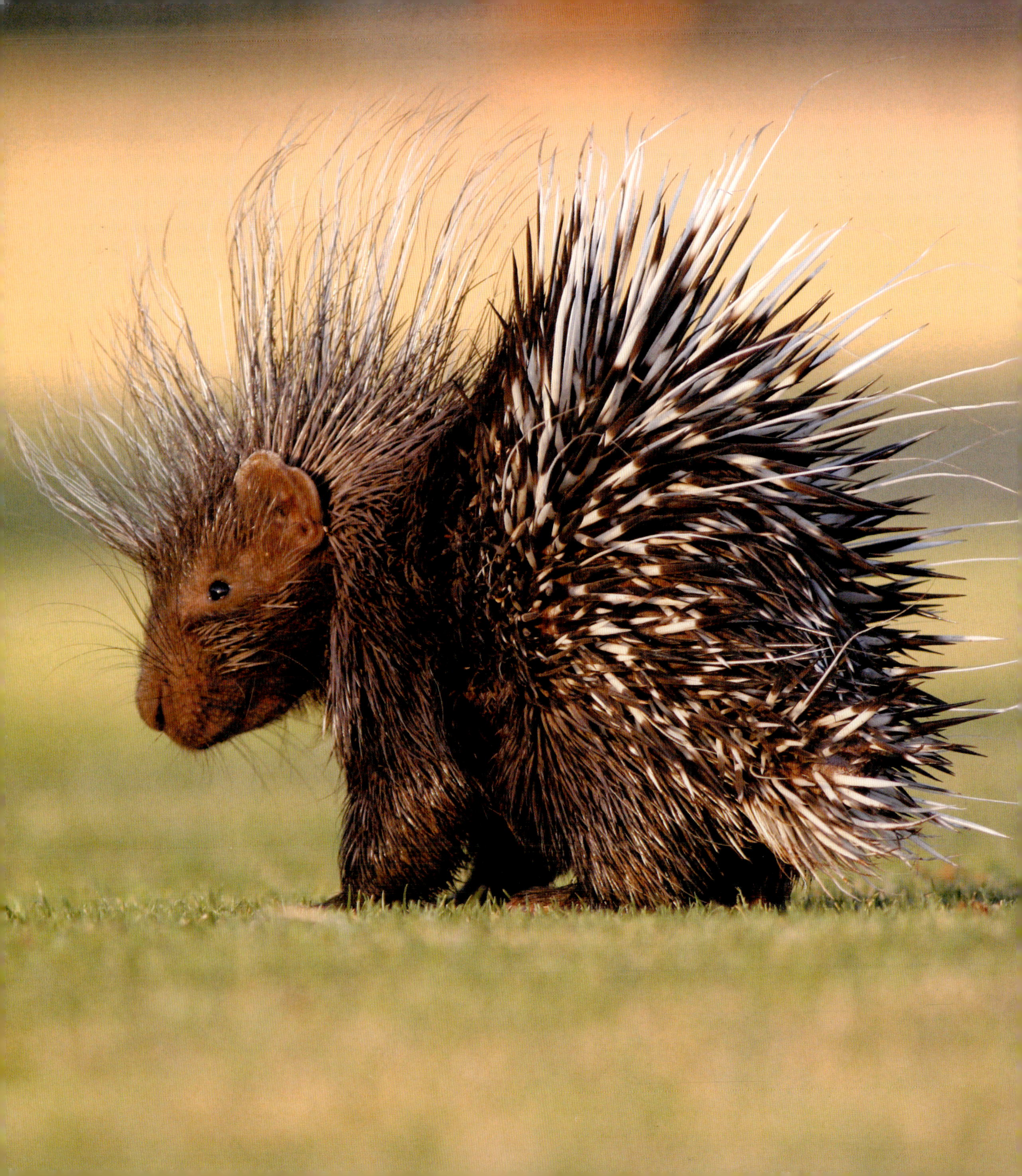

Spiky bums

Some animals have spikes on their bums or on their tails. If attacked, they aim the sharp spikes at their attackers.

African porcupines walk along with their tail spikes down but can quickly raise them if threatened.

A group of dinosaurs known as stegosaurs had sharp spikes at the tips of their tails. They could swing their tails at attackers like giant spiked clubs.

Fast and fat tails

Goannas use their long thin tails like whips. If attackers get too close, they whip their tails into the attackers' eyes.

Some geckos have thick tails in which they store fat. This helps them get through times when food is hard to find. If attacked, they can also drop their tails and leave them as wriggling meals so they can get away. Then they grow a new one.

Strange bums

Snails only have one opening to their shells. This means snails don't have tails. Instead the poo comes out over their heads. Imagine if humans were made this way!

Sea anemones have only one hole in their bodies. This hole is both the mouth and the bum. Food goes in and when it is all digested the poo is spat out the same hole.

Fact files

African Bombardier Beetle (Stenaptinus insignis)
This small beetle uses its cannon-like tail to squirt hot liquid in the face of its enemies, mainly ants. It can aim the squirt gun in any direction and can fire it off up to 70 times in one go. This gives it enough time to unfold its wings and flap away. It makes a "pop" sound every time its cannon goes off.

Bigbelly Seahorse (Hippocampus abdominalis)
Seahorses feed by sitting very still in coral or seaweed. When schools of small shrimp swim close by, seahorses suck them up one at a time with their long tube mouths. The males raise the babies in special fat pouches on their stomachs.

Rattlesnake (Crotalus)
Rattlesnakes live in North and South America. They have a deadly bite. They use fangs to inject strong venom that destroys flesh, and causes swelling and internal bleeding. They only bite as a last resort and are not dangerous if left alone. Most people are bitten trying to catch or kill these snakes.

Sea Anemone (Anthothoe albocincta)
Sea anemones have rings of tentacles around their mouths. The tentacles have lots of stinging cells to catch small animals. Anemones can reproduce by growing small copies of themselves or dividing in half. It would be like us growing a twin brother or sister out our armpit!

Sea Cucumber (Bohadschia argus)

Sea cucumbers are related to starfish. They have mouths like a head of cauliflower that they use to lick up scraps of food and dead animal remains off the sea floor. Some species even have pairs of fish known as pearlfish that live in sea cucumbers' bottoms!

Striped Skunk (Mephitis mephitis)

This skunk species feeds on insects, worms, snails, fruit, grains and nuts. It also hunts moles, rats and squirrels. One of its favourite foods is bees. It attacks the hive then eats the bees as they swarm out. Most predators leave skunks alone. Their main predators are great horned owls. Like all birds, the owl probably doesn't have a strong sense of smell.

Thick-tailed Gecko (Underwoodisaurus milii)

These beautiful lizards live in the deserts of Australia. They come out at night to hunt insects with their sticky tongues. They keep their huge eyes clean by licking them. They are also called the barking gecko because their calls sound like a small dog barking.

Trapdoor Spider (Misgolas)

The burrow of a trapdoor spider is lined with soft silk. With a thick door it makes a nice place to live, protected from the weather outside. A female trapdoor spider lives in the same burrow for all its life, sometimes for as long as 20 years! Males move about looking for mates.

Whale Shark (Rhincodon typus)

Whale sharks are the biggest fish in the world. They are as long as a bus! They look scary but are gentle giants. They have small teeth and only eat the tiniest animals known as plankton, as well as small fish, squid and shrimp. They live in tropical seas all around the world.

Glossary

burrow: a hole made in the ground by an animal for shelter

digestion: when the body breaks down food before absorbing it and using it for energy

fangs: pointed teeth

gland: an organ that makes a substance needed by the body

paralysed: when something is unable to move, even if it wants to

plankton: tiny animals and plants that drift in water

poisonous: containing poison, a harmful substance

predator: any animal that survives by feeding on other animals

tentacles: long flexible parts of an animal used to touch or hold

tropical: a hot and humid environment

venomous: an animal that can make, and pass on, venom

Index

A
African bombardier beetle 30
ant 21, 30

B
bee 20, 31
Bigbelly seahorse 30
bombardier beetle 16, 30
bull ant 21

C
caterpillar 18

D
dinosaur 25
dolphin 15

G
gecko 27, 31
goanna 26
grasshopper 7
great horned owl 31

L
lemur 10

M
mole 31
monkey 12

P
peacock 10
pearlfish 31
plankton 31, 32
porcupine 25

R
rat 31
rattlesnake 7, 30

S
scorpion 22
sea anemone 28, 30
sea cucumber 17, 31
seahorse 12, 30
shark 14, 31
shrimp 30, 31
skunk 18, 31
snail 28, 31
spider 8, 9, 31
squirrel 31
starfish 31
stegosaurus 25
stingray 23
stink bug 18

T
thick-tailed gecko 31
trapdoor spider 9, 31

W
whale 15
whale shark 31
worm 31